52
Golden Pieces

52 Golden Pieces

All illustrations by the Haitian artist Patrick Gaspard.

ISBN: 979-8-9888051-2-0 (hardcover)
         979-8-9888051-0-6 (paperback)
         979-8-9888051-1-3 (ebook)

Printed in the United States of America

52
Golden Pieces

Jean René Bazin PierrePierre

Table of Contents

Preamble

The smart thief

One day a thief, having set his aim on a specific house and observed carefully the daily habits of its occupants, set himself ready, one clear morning, to execute his plan. In the house there were Mum and Dad, five siblings and one visiting cousin. The eldest of the siblings was a twenty-three year (23) old strong young man, actively involved in his college wrestling team. The others were eight years old (8), a set of five-year (5) old twins and a toddler. The cousin of close to seventeen years (17) of age was visiting from his high school recess. So the smart thief waited till the parents leave for their day's work and made his way to the back door he knew was always left unlocked.

When he entered the house, tell me who is he going to neutralize first and foremost?

Just like that house our mother, the church is under attack by thieves inside and out. Foolish beyond belief it would be for anyone to just move into another house…

Junie, My Angel

Junie my angel
Junie my sweet dove
Come close and dispel
My nightmares of love
Junie my promise
Junie torn apart
Come so I can kiss
All the scars that keep us apart

Junie my angel
Junie peaceful soul
Come out of your shell
Return what you stole
Junie my soulmate
Junie my sweetheart
Come and reinstate
Its most treasured part.
Come open the cage
You should have the key
Or break the bondage
It's not that risky
And start a new stage
Where we can write our love story

Junie meek and mild
Junie all alone
Come my blessed child
Come and take your throne
Reign over this land
Parched and desolate
Your time is at hand
Come and change its fate.

Junie fair lady
Junie my godsent
My sole melody
Come give your consent
End this tragedy
My plane long started its descent.

Junie my angel
Junie please be bold
People will come tell
What they know of old
Don't buy any tale
That could make you cold
Their stories are stale
I long paid my toll.

Junie my sunshine
Junie my blue sky
Junie child on mine
Junie sweet and shy,
Be my angel fine
Please, don't let Heaven pass us by

Junie my angel
Junie my refrain
Come write our gospel
And so crush my pain
Open up your mind
Wash your thoughts away
Deep inside you'll find
What the Lord has laid
For our souls to bind
And journey His way

Junie lucky charm
Junie my lifeguard
Open up your arms
Do not disregard
This poor castaway
With gesturing cries
If you go away
He will surely lie down and die.

To Marijune,

Sun and Moon

The moon said to the sun
I'll catch you, I'll catch you.
So tirelessly she spun
After the dazzling hue.

The sun steadily sprang
In the sky faded blue
And in galactic slang
Replied I love you too.

And the earth all-tipsy
By the relentless chase
Wishes never to see
The ending of this race.

The sky would never bless
This all forbidden love
For when one is at rest
The other shines above…

Pray the Creator
Our love to attune
For without His favor
We'll be like sun and moon.

The Chosen Ones

We had our shares of ups and downs,
We had our share of joys and frowns
But through it all; sun, snow and rain,
Right there, by His side we remained.

Oh there were times we felt stranded,
Cursed, dejected, empty-handed
But even in the darkest nights
We never lost of Him the sight.

His eyes of love melting us all
Kept in our hearts the blessed call
And His Spirit, our souls stirring,
Gave peace and joy everlasting.

So there we went in this minefield
We call this world. But with His shield
Of love and peace and harmony
Conquered hatred hegemony.

We have His Word that it will be
Better the other side of sea.
So we press on through sorrow, pain
Even when we don't comprehend.

But many times our faith flickered;
Poor human beings we grew weaker.
But when we read His life anew,
It reminded us what to do.

For in His Father He trusted
Till the last hour though busted.
And like a lamb He shed His life
So that in turn we have no strife.

So heed His Word, do as He says,
Follow in His path unafraid
For as He won the victory
We too will go down history

As chosen ones who so remained
Despite loads of sorrow and pain
And their own share of joys and frowns,
But will be wearing golden crowns.

Blizzard

'Twas a cold winter's night
And no soul was in sight.
The sky heavy and gray
Had just melted our way
And left the whole borough
Under blankets of snow.

On that January night
That soft and spongy blight
Was all over the town,
Spreading cold, spreading frown
On every tree and branch,
Every hole, every trench.

You could go for long miles
And find cars in long files
But nothing was moving,
Mot a bird was singing.
Nature lied down all crushed,
Even the wind had hushed.

So the City crippled
Was facing the triple
Of amount of snowfall
Since one can last recall…
It was just not ready
To face this comedy.

In the middle of streets
As high as many feet
You'd barely recognize
The many cars chastised;
Because their drivers dared
They ended up…nowhere

And so the night stood still
The décor was surreal.
Of the street lamp the glow
Had a steady halo
Giving the whole picture
A heavenly texture.

The rare sounds were muffled.
You'd move in a shuffle
For the snow was so high
But still soft and yet dry
Enough to stick around
Many days on the ground.

The streets looked so different,
In the air was no scent.
You might just as well be,
Weighing all that you see,
Just off some rocket jet
On some other planet.

No attempt at your car
Live you near, live you far.
It would not move the least;
The roads did not exist.
'Twas a spotless white sea
As far as eyes could see.

And you felt this mixture
Of sadness and pleasure
For if this pile of snow
Will stop life tomorrow,
You, you picture instead
Tough shoveling ahead

For you know that for now
You'll rearrange somehow
All your plans rendered vain
And ride the "7" train.
For on a night like this
All City lives just ceased.

Sunday

There is something in a Sunday,
This so unordinary day,
When skies are blue
And sun shines through
Within a meek heart come what may.

There is something in a Sunday,
When all the faithful come and lay
At their Lord's feet
Weary spirits
And in unison sing and pray.

There is something in a Sunday,
When souls leap high in a hooray
For then God's touch
Gives them back much
Courage and strength when skies are gray.

For to the humble souls who pray,
Spring, summer fall or winter days,
At each sunrise
God hears their sighs
And makes every day a Sunday.

Harvest

The wheat and weeds of this world
Hand in hand will grow,
From one day by nature curled
By the Gardener sowed.

The wheat and weeds of this world
Always live in pain;
What to one's seen as a pearl,
The others disdain.

The wheat and weeds of this world
Carry their sorrow
The Spirit by them both furled,
Pants under their blows.

The wheat and weeds of this world
Will part at the end,
Swiftly they will be unfurled
And finally gleaned.

The wheat and weeds of this world
Will go separate ways;
To hell or the gate of pearls
As the bible says.

The Angelus

Slowly the orange disc slips in the western sea
And the skies mournfully miss daylight already.
The silence peacefully comes the whole world cover
And a veil of shadows spreads its wings all over.
Within hearts of goodwill the Spirit awakens,
Just like deer to water, bends towards the Heavens.
Humble and serene brows in prayerful posture
Come give thanks and praises to the Lord, who nurtures,
For each other, for health and nourishing pasture.

In the air comes ringing the blessed Angelus,
Echoing in the skies like a morose chorus.
It permeates the souls of every beating heart
Regardless of belief that might set them apart.
The divine sound of love calling all human beings
To rest from daily chores and in faith their hearts bring
To the sole Provider, the eternal Father,
Maker of all that's good, of all lives the Keeper.
The God who lovingly watches over His flock
Who shepherds them safely from epoch to epoch.
For in sheer unison, the chime of the vesper
Stirs in all human hearts the love of the Father.

On Jordan's Bank

As I walked nonchalant on Jordan's bank one day,
I saw the usual crowd carrying down their prey.
The people were busy doing their daily chores
Working hard judging by the run down from their pores.

The sun golden brilliance made nature look lovely,
Radiating like a bride, passionate and jolly.
The birds were so many on the branches of trees,
That those wished, as it seemed, this big load they could ease.

As I tried from this scene not to be hypnotized,
I caught glimpse of a crowd riveted, mesmerized,
Listening to a Man, rather tall and handsome,
Speaking, from what I heard, of another kingdom.

He said happy are they who suffer in this world
For up in the Heavens their cries are always heard.
And to every goodness people on earth will sow,
In the Kingdom of God, sure their harvest will grow.

He spoke with such a voice that carried in echo.
At times from His body you could perceive a glow.
I tried to make my way much closer to the Man
Hoping to see His face or even touch His hand.

I fought with all my strength and managed finally,
Shoved by a crazed young man screaming: "Now I can see",
To be at one arm's length from this this Jordan Preacher,
Who, as I just gathered, was to be our Leader.

He spoke of a young man who took all the money
His father had for him, went on a spending spree.
Then being in bankruptcy and on a foreign land,
Was afraid to return and his father offend.

He paused for an instant, turned His face toward me.
At that solemn moment looked at me peacefully.
I gazed within these Eyes piercing me to the core,
What came over me then changed me forever more…

PS

Many books were written on this Man's achievements,
No one wrote about His concealed accomplishments…
Lord, make that if one day of my life I meet You
Just like on Jordan's bank I fall in love with You.

The Hand of God

From every walk, from every race,
From every smile upon a face
The hand of God to His children
Always comes straight from their brethren.

It comes often, it comes in need,
It comes in due time, good old seed
That planted well within the hearts
Should spread around the divine Spark.

To every smile, to every word,
Written, sung, spoken or uttered,
A direct result is obtained
Reflecting the love of God's hand.

From every walk, every embrace,
Every kind word or smiley face,
The love of god to his children
Showers the world down to its end.

Fickle and Flighty

Every day, every hour life brings you your request,
What spoken, what hidden, how deep within your chest
But every time a door opens to your favor,
Too fickle and flighty, you lose all your ardor.

And the years brought the pain and the tears, the lessons
But the shouts of wisdom you sadly perceived none.
And from the mouths you kissed you ignored the clamor:
"So fickle and flighty, why you lost your ardor?"

So there it came one day that in some unknown place,
By a just twist of fate you fell in her embrace.
There, kept under her spell, you sang like a tenor:
"Though fickle and flighty, I won't lose my ardor."

Every day, every hour life with us plays its game
And what you so dispensed, to you it sends the same.
Just when you got the grip of a steady candor,
Fickle, flighty in turn, she lost all her ardor.

To Erjola,

The Good Order of Things

The good order of things should never be disturbed.
The divine way of things should remain unperturbed:
I wake up at daylight,
The thought of you surface
And though you're out of sight
In my heart you take place.

The good order of things will always entertain,
The way that long ago they were set right and plain:
Two hearts beating as one,
Playing one melody
Exquisite, uncommon,
Strong proof of His mercy.

The good order of things, we will have to preserve,
The good order of things demands that I reserve
Your loving hand in mine
While walking side by side
Towards this joy divine
And in His love abide.

The good order of things though sometimes uncertain,
The good order of things in His hands will remain.
We may lose heart one day
We'll never drift apart
For we stayed in His way,
Secured things from the start.
The good order of things is like a dream come true,
Each time you say to me: "My Beba, I love you."

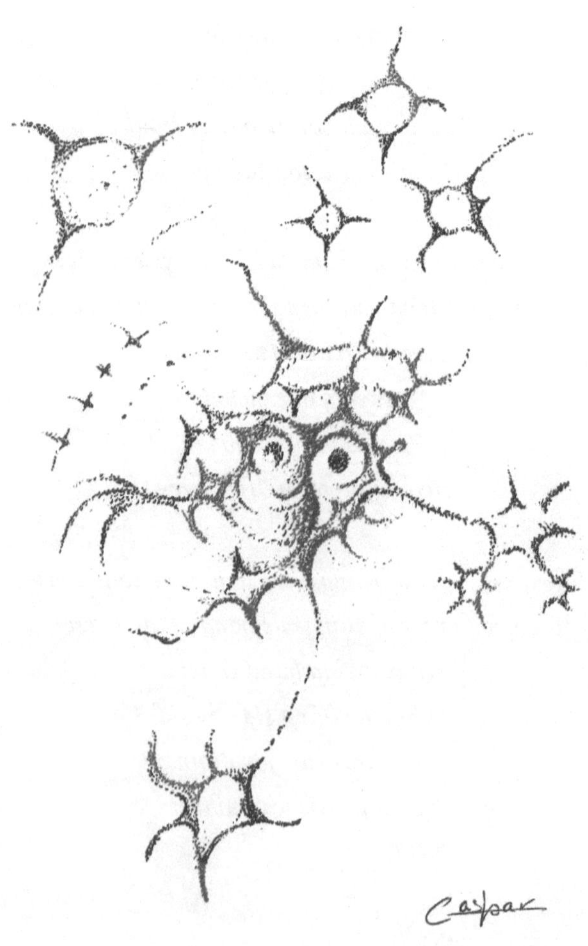

Carpe Diem

Don't put till tomorrow
What you can do today.
Your chances will narrow,
The prize may drift away.

Don't dwell on days ahead,
Daily gives of your best.
Always carry your lead,
The Lord will do the rest.

The Hereafter

The great veil of the hereafter
One day to us will uncover,
As baffling as now it all seems,
Why we should hold pain in esteem.

For perturbing as it may sound,
In religions the world around,
What entertains our bodies
Are the spirit worst enemies.

Funny how these two entities,
Paired to form all humanities,
Can be bound to become just one
But yet in common carry none.

But as human forward we go
Choosing which to allow to grow;
The body with vices galore
Or the spirit we should restore.

This very basic dilemma
Of the world affects the karma
And one so painfully ponders
The cause of the world disasters…

At every level of matter,
At every tear, every laughter,
The part of you that you honor
Will make you loser or winner.

Hurry, exercise your free will,
This privilege is ours still.
Choose while life's yet given to us,
Choose to be free, choose to be just.

For as baffling as it may seem,
Despite the body hungry screams,
One day we will soon discover
The whole truth in the hereafter.

For Your Love Only

Only for the kindness of you
Will I open my heart's treasure.
Only for this love so brand new
Will I blossom behind measure.
I will reveal my fondest dreams,
Will unveil my most precious themes
That all the while, when you so chose,
My heart gladly to you disclosed.

But you wonder do I love you,
Do I feel the divine treasure?
And senselessly you think I do
Refuse of your arms the capture…

I'll let you on a secret
That no one thus far has heard yet…
Before, way before your "hello"
Your heartbeats in mine had echoed
And all the while you stood afar
I swear I saw my lucky star.
Keep it to yourself, my jolie,
I love you for your love only.

The Loving Touch

The loving touch seeks no reward.
Timid, it comes and brings a hand,
A hand it lands with no regard
To the effect often obtained.

It comes with love just to offset
The worries and cares of the day.
Upon its wings of light garnet
There's zeal to dissipate your gray.

In return it begs for a smile
Or a happy glow from your eyes.
But always it settles meanwhile
For a lessening of your sighs.

The loving touch seeks forgiveness
For the wrongs it tries to atone
And it deeply feels the distress,
Of the abuse it hears the tone.

And so it comes, bearing solace,
Hoping to soothe your every ill
For the loving touch is a grace
Sent by the good Lord to us still.

Christmas Gift

Like children we rejoice
All through the Christmas time.
Like children, with one voice,
We carol along chimes.
Like children, on that eve,
We wait for the dear Lord.
Like children we receive
Gifts and presents galore.

Like children the next day
We feast and play great deal.
Like children, come what may,
The love of Christ we feel.
Like children, after all
The festive times are gone,
Like children, big or small,
We leave the Babe alone.

And in the poor manger
Where He lies for us all
He goes on to shiver,
Cast out of all recall…
Could we, with hearts of love,
Warm His tender body
Since He came from above
All ills to remedy?

Like children every year
We trample all our toys.
Then next Christmas appears
Bringing back other joys…
May the gift of our souls,
Gentle, meek, loving, kind,
Be our best gift to hold
Within our hearts and minds.

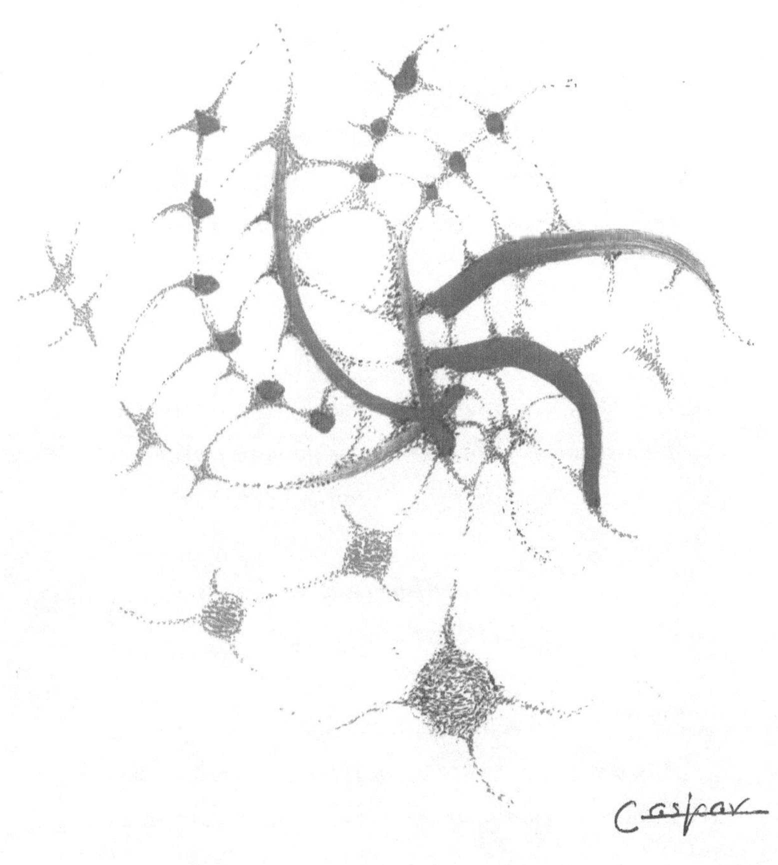

Have Faith

You're all alone
And drowning in your grief
For your friends have all gone
To your great disbelief
And the world around you takes a shade of dark gray
And your will for living has just faded away.

Sometimes in life,
Often with no warning,
You come across the path
Of painful happenings
That shatter all your thoughts of a world made of love,
Shake your faith in the words He has once spoken of.

Have faith in the Lord,
Believe in the Lord,
He'll carry us through with the strength of His love
And just when you think there's no hope from above,
Remain faithful to the Lord.

So Father we come
And kneel at Your feet,
Let us feel the awesome
Power of Your Spirit
And bearing our burdens in the name of Your Son,
We'll witness Your great Love till our days here are done.

Listen

Always get to the point
But to others be kind.
A simple trade of mind
Can often disappoint.

Listen with great patience
To others be proper.
Show the other speaker
That they too have essence.

It's always very rude
To speak before your turn.
The truth that you might learn
Your mind, would just elude.

For the same ears you lend
To someone in sorrow,
Before it's tomorrow
Your voicing may attend.

Remember talk is cheap,
Not even worth a pence.
But always with silence
Great wisdom you will reap.

The Key

I got a key to my door,
A door I closed long ago.
Behind it, just as before,
Lie treasures that I only know.

I got a key to my heart,
My heart where pure love's stirring.
It was molded from the start
By the Maker of everything.

I got a key to my soul,
My soul of many tears filled;
Tears of joy and sorrow old,
All that at your feet I just spilled.

So here's the key to my door,
The door of my heart and soul;
I will be yours from the core
If you can only find the hole.

Duel

The roll of drums comes loud and clear,
The roll of drums sounds awfully near.
But it persists,
Clenching the fists
Of the fighters more than ready.

The roll of drums never misses,
Surges after all the kisses
The combatants,
Wives and infants
Exchange before the assembly.

The roll of drums, strong and steady
Spread its lugubrious melody
And in the fog
Even the hogs
Put a halt to their gluttony.

The roll of drums though so sturdy,
The roll of drums is not merry.
It fails to hide
Vain human pride,
The root of this insanity.

The roll of drums will keep going
And the drummers won't miss a thing;
Not a mere blow
Given too low
Will fail to mark its harmony.

The roll of drums will reach its top
Then suddenly comes to a stop
When at the end
Only one stands
In the gray dawn of Tuscany.

Honey Moon Song

O come my lovely child,
Come rest yourself by me.
See how the night is mild
And the stars are many.

They're here to celebrate
And bless our first embrace.
They shine as to relate
To us their borrowed grace.

Always they'll remind us,
If ever we forget,
In case we are devious,
Of the time we first met.

So the vows that we swore
To us before the Lord,
More than ever before
Should seal our accord.

For the world is ready
To smother in our hearts
By words full of envy
What flame made us sweethearts.

Come, come my blessed child,
Restore yourself in my.
Soon the moon will have miled
And the stars will all flee.

To my son, Joël

The Last Time

For the last time I will tell you
What for you should be déjà vu.
It is simple yet essential,
Important, even primordial
That you listen to what I say
For this time I'll be on my way.

There will be time, rather quite near
When you will face your inner fear.
Time dark and sad, heavy, painful
When the least pleasure's distasteful.
When the fresh air, so caressing
Don't even stir any feeling
From within your distraught spirit;
When your heart and hers do not meet.

There, in the corner of your room,
On the rocks savoring your gloom,
You will ponder repeatedly
The reasons why you're so lonely
And you will gaze at your window,
Regurgitating your sorrow,
You will regret so bitterly
The time when she was your jolie.

See life teaches to us humans
Bitter lessons more than often
But then we go on senselessly
Back to repeat the same follies.
I often picture the adults,
Even the elders they consult,
Carrying cross with sobbing tears
That they built up in younger years.

And so we go, and so we go
Stepping on the thorns that we sow'.
We cry for help, call for a truce
But we go on changing the truths.
And with the conscience kept at cool
We freely break the golden rules
That we were taught from the nipple,
Long time before we were crippled.

It's often hard to realize
How close we've gotten to the prize.
What is today on your pillow
May depart from you tomorrow
And you'll be left lonely, stranded,
Just cause you took her for granted.

So win her love, secure your joy.
If love's a game, she's not a toy.
An ounce of feeling invested
Results in kisses harvested
For remember this golden truth
Which quite often eludes the youth:
A woman is like a flower;
Once with tender care you shower
Her gentle and fragile petals
In your arms naturally she falls.

I Love You

I love you with a borrowed heart
I love you loud and clear,
I love you sweet, I love you tart,
I love your peach, my dear.

I love you when the day is done,
I love you when it rains,
I love you when the sunlight's shone
On this God fearing land.

I love you for what you offer,
I love you or your smile
That sweetens me like no other
Has done for a long while.

I love you any given day
That I become aware
That through this life of disarray
I have your steady care.

I love you in my sleep,
Kissing your lovely face
And treasuring the feel I reap;
Fears of nightmares erased.

I love the words you speak,
I love you for your touch,
I love you proud, I love you meek,
When my advice you brush.

I love you when it's hot or cold,
Riveted by your charm,
I love you when my hand you hold
With your touch soft and warm.

I love you then, I'll love you still
When my work here is done.
And I'll love you beyond my will
When my soul will have flown.

Equilibrium

So you return and heartily try to amend
Another living soul your wrong deeds once offend'.
And deep within yourself you feel satisfaction,
Immense sense of goodness, divine restoration…

It's just that your true self, the spirit within you,
Avows its counterpart, offers it what is due;
The first humbling himself blooms in divine treasures,
The other consenting, replaces lost measures.

The Merciful

And when it's all over, Master, we'll come to You,
Standing there with our load, bewildered by the view.
Will You, Father of Love, will You, so merciful,
Will You deny yourself, the part we call here soul?

You promised us Heaven, a peaceful place of rest
But simply in return expect from us the best
That we can truly be; striving with good and bad,
Knowing that our deeds will make us happy or sad.

You being so merciful, we'll be at Your mercy.
You being the Font of love, we'll be so love hungry
For nothing else can feed this part that You create
For from Your inner self gladly we emanate.

If You see dear Father, that the load we bring back,
For some mundane reasons, Your divine love they lack,
Have pity, my dear Lord, have pity on us all,
We rest on Your Spirit despite our many falls.

Only then, my dear Lord, absolved and forgiven,
We will taste in the core the lost gift now regained.
And once again Master, You'll do what You do best,
You'll forgive Your children though they all fail Your tests.

So when it's all over, we'll put our trust in You
And we'll stand there ready for You to make us new.
But will You, Font of Love, will You, Font of Mercy,
Will You watch Your children for Your Love go hungry?

M.G.M.M.

O come my lovely one,
Come and see how undone
This heart you once forsook
Remains without the brook
Of love and tenderness
That you are, my princess.

O come my beloved,
See how perfectly made
The bed of scented rose
With the finest of clothes,
All picked at your measure,
Your soul to recapture,

O come my angel fine,
Come again and be mine.
Long, long, so long ago
My heart to yours echoed.
Come therefore, please return,
His love plea, do not spurn.

To Marijune,

The Taste of Things That Passed

The bitter sweet,
The all-cherished,
The painful treats,
The unfinished,
Each time they ring
Deep in your ears
They always bring
Unpleasant tears…

Will you ever forget this love,
Will you finally get rid of
This kneeling feeling that her name
Imposes on your heart she tamed?...

The lonely beat,
Impoverished,
Who did not meet
His so cherished
Dances with slings
Of lonesome fears
To the beguine
Of you, my dear.

How Do I Love Thee

How to express the way I feel,
How to entirely reveal
The nature of the euphoria
Your brown eyes sow on my aura?

How can I truthfully transmit
That in the realm of the spirit
The love you steadily pour out
Impounds my soul without a doubt?

See, words convey the way we feel,
They can describe what's fake and real
But they remain cold and petty
When they merge into the fairy.

How can I open up my heart
And let you know that from the start,
You swan dove on my misery
And made my world bright and merry?

How can I truly voice out,
Find the right words to help me shout
That without you my world withers?...
Well, let's not misuse the others.

The Mission

I don't write to entertain
But rather to enlighten.
Though the first brings much laughter,
The body needed healer,
The second brings to the soul
True wisdom to make it whole.

I don't write to entertain,
My thoughts I write bold and plain.
I would much rather offer
To my lost and poor brothers
Solace in the strives instead,
When they'll face the loads ahead.

I don't write to entertain
But hope so much to sustain
In this tedious, dreary walk,
With my readers a plain talk.
For tomorrow, laugh or learn,
That bright light we'll all discern.

The Voice of God

The voice of God I heard
Telling me: "Go fetch the others,
Go all over the world
And spread the news to all your brothers!"

In my hesitation
I shied the task entrusted to me.
A world of temptations
To my lost self added misery.

So then the voice of God
Lifted the veil upon my blindness
And out of my pod
Of other grains I could see the zest.

And strengthened by the crowd
I started by telling the good news.
It came out clear and loud
That God is Love so love we should choose.

Funeral

How sublime it appears at the end of the path;
The Lord sends His angels to get us on the raft,
Leading us safely home where we always belong,
Home where our Father expects us for so long.

But O funeral! How depressing and dreadful
Are the long hours spent, sitting there, pitiful,
Receiving friends and foes expressing: "I'm sorry",
When that old second part you can't wait to bury.

My Day

As I woke up today
Your Face shone upon me.
"Let's go and make a day",
You said to me gently.

So with You I went on
Through my day's ups and downs.
When the burdens pressed on
You chased away my frowns.

You led me peacefully,
I leaned on Your strong arm
And went on happily;
Gave to the world my charm.

I recall You told me:
"Show kindness all around
And from your enemy
You will see love abound."

I tell of Your mercy
To my brethren around,
Remind them constantly
For them Your love profound.

Through sun or rain or snow,
All life intemperance,
I carry my sorrow,
Hope for deliverance.

Heavy is the day's load,
Intense the sufferings
But since my hand You hold
They have different meaning.

As I lay down today
Your Face shone upon me:
"Let us call it a day",
You smiled to me gently.

On The Journey

Before the end of this here day
There'll be a door on your journey,
A door that opens on the way,
Where you can rest in His mercy.

You'll enter in. you'll be greeted.
Be kind to the ones you meet there.
Don't take anything for granted
And they will treat you fair and square.

If any one addresses you
Reply to them with a bright smile.
Be gentle in all that you do
And their customs do not defile.

Offer your help to the widows,
To the lonely ease the sorrow
But to the bold and the proud ones
Offer your service more than once.

But if this world of temptations
Ensnares the fibers of your flesh
And if the least of your actions
Seems to keep your soul in a mesh.

And if the demons within you
Caused your zealous heart to be lured
And in your faithfulness though true
You lose the guidance of His Word

Rely solely on His kindness
And on the strength of His Spirit.
His strong Love and His forgiveness
Will redeem all your demerits.

To Marijune,

Pathways

Down the hallways of life, tread a man and his soul,
The hallways where we all struggle to take control
Of the ups and downs of living,
Of fate and love disheartening.
They talk in silent sobs of broken love affairs
Where words of forever and you and I don't pair.
But lightly they both tread
And their sadness is fed
By each and everyone with their soul that they meet,
Walking down the hallways born by the same Spirit.

Down the pathways of life where we only meet once.
O life, O life, why do you still our loved ones?

PS

It's been a sheer blessing to have known in my life
A sweet angel like you, of gentleness so rife.

Happy Birthday

And the sun slowly rose,
Made that beautiful day.
This one among all those
Celebrates your birthday.
So you open your eyes,
Suddenly it hits you;
This is a day for prize
That the Lord made for you.

So you kneel down and pray
To the One and only
Spirit who faithfully
Watches over your way.
You thank Him that so far
From all His multitude
He has made you a star;
So you show gratitude.

Your face lights up with joy,
We all say we love you.
You blushed and then destroy
The wraps red, gold and blue.
You marveled at your gifts,
So far no one failed you.
We are all finalists
At that game déjà vu.

I wish you all the best,
May your life be fruitful!
Remember, serve the rest,
You'll be paid plentiful.
Life remains a journey
For the rich or needy,
Love, faith and charity,
All you need to carry.

How I Wish

The little joys that life bestows,
Like when I hold you in my arms.
The little joys erase the blows
When I fall, stricken by your charms.

The little thrills that I can sense,
Like when I hold your pretty face,
The thrilling ups and the descents
Roller coast my heart in its pace.

The many words you can whisper
Resound over within my mind,
But none can compare in flavor
To when you say you miss me blind.

If It Were

If it were that one day,
Wish it wouldn't be Monday,
That from such a sudden
You'd become a maiden
And decide that anew
It would be just us two
And dedicate to me your entire family,
Oh what a thrill it'd be!

If it were that one day
Hope it'd be a Tuesday.
I always love to say
That on this day I'd pray
And with faith will obtain
Anything I demand.
So if it were I said
That with me you'd be laid.
Oh why I'm so afraid!

If it were that one day
We will have walked that way
Leading to the altar
Hoping it's no too far.
That you'd answer: "I do,
Till death apart us do"
To the Lord's minister
Blessing our foyer,
Oh what a sweet affair!

But never came that day,
God knows how much I prayed.
You chose the other way
And threw my hopes away.
Life is made of surprise.
I did not compromise
Value and principles
Those are strong and simple.
Oh what a heavy blow!

Peace Within

Do you know my sweet Lord, what you did to my life?
You ask me to trust You, that You'd send me a wife.
Though I don't feel deprived of human affection
I often feel the weight of this situation.

I made many mistakes in life, I must admit.
Sometimes I think they are tiny blocks of concrete
That You superimpose in building of my life;
Though I don't want to plead on my failures behalf.

But in this hurricane, these tormented waters,
Though the winds were so strong and mighty their powers,
You raised Your Hand, O Lord, to my inner fury
Commanded to slow down; the waves became steady.

So deep within my soul, O Lord, my God, remain.
Do not permit ever my spirit to refrain
From the delightful joy it finally obtained;
That peace that You promise, that faith that moves mountains.

For only divine peace often by us ignored
Can lead to the graces for which we so implore.
Grace of a better me, grace of a better life
And in the near future, of course grace of a wife.

Human Pride

Human pride is a poison,
The worst of deadly potion,
Anchored well within the hearts,
Smothering love that imparts
Life in creatures born divine.
It severs them from the Vine,
The Source of all that's good
And the teachings that they should
Uphold as life instructions
To avoid all confusions.

As smart as the pestilence
From which it takes provenance,
It often remains hidden
Deep in the heart smallest den
Then springs like the wildest beast
To rob from the very least
The all-divine, bequeathed peace,
Prelude of heavenly bliss
To the creatures who know how
To bend the knee and head bow.

Human pride is a poison.
Let's then make the distinction
'Tween the forefathers deceits
And our deep own conceits.
For a human always errs
That justifies not the airs
Dictating the behavior
Of shunning our Savior.
He the Truth, the Life, the Way.
From His path let us not stray.

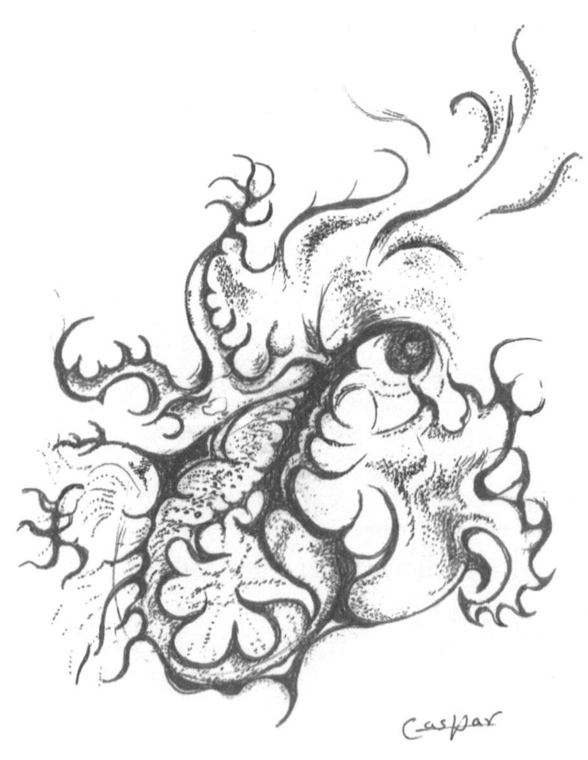

Return

I miss your lovely eyes and your beautiful smile,
I long to hear your voice resounding in my ears,
The softness of your hands; all for which my heart cheers
Causing that around you is where I want to while.

But in my heart, my love, the quivering reveal
The awful hours spent when you are not with me.
The days drag endlessly and deep inside I feel
The misery until you come back already.

But when you will return what will unveil my heart?
Speechless I will remain, quivering but jovial
And my eyes full of you, my lovely, better part,
Will they ever reveal my love to you at all?

But if ever my dear, you'd find me cold, distant,
Don't go making a scene with your mind wandering.
Remember that always away from you being,
I can't help my poor heart; I suffer and lament.

In Your Vicinity

When you are by my side, doing what you do best,
Just being you, that is, right there I feel my chest
Fighting hard to contain the turbulence in me.
Be it your lovely face, your smile, your lips maybe,

Every little detail comes to disturb my peace.
My poor self, mesmerized declares without notice
To be at your beckons whensoever you please,
To remain by your side and so suffer your tease.

Jesus, Gift of The Father

There is always along the path of daily life
Someone who lovingly helps us carry our cross.
He or she usually acts on our behalf,
When comes the next burden, helps us to get across.

You can never discern who today it will be;
This will always remain in life a mystery.
But we can rest assured of the promise He made;
When the sun is too hot to put us in His shade.

One day Jerusalem became the center stage
Of a drama the world up to this day, appall.
Condemned and crucified; all this in such a rage,
Though at his accusers He never swung at all.

The same intensity of rage and cruelty
That this scene illustrates, remains for us truly
Essential instructions of life's deep mysteries;
Parables in His life, He offers a series.

One is underlined here, the one of cross bearing.
Of this life's sufferings it carries a meaning.
But just as from Cyrene His help our Lord received
From any walk of life ours' always retrieved.

But we should not when faced with any life turmoil
To the Heavens above display such annoyance.
And if we were praying, our knees on the soil,
Should not get up angry, devoid of all patience,

At the Lord Almighty always willing to prove
That our every wound He is willing to soothe...
So trust the One above. He never in His ways
Fails to carry the soul who only to Him prays.

He is the life, He says, the One who animates
And all our endeavors, always investigates.
He knows our weakness and before we appeal
To Him He already provides for us a deal.

So go to Him always, in faith make your demands
For if our father of flesh our needs attends,
With divine compassion, the heavenly Father
Did better. He gave us Jesus-Christ, our Savior.

Just a Thought

And so there'll be, in days ahead,
A flow of love running with stead
From my heart to you, my Chérie.

You opened up its every door
And unlike anything before
Its ticking's fierce and yet merry.

Once in a while, when He beckons,
The Lord gives blessings in seconds
To rearrange a stagnant life.

Then all grateful, down on my knees,
I beg of you, oh baby, please,
Will you accept to be my wife?

Knight's Confession

While you were sleeping this morning,
With the angels doing their thing,
I tiptoed in your life, my dear,
With my armor, my shield, my spear.

While you were sleeping I remained,
Keeping guard on your meek domain.
Not even a lonesome scarecrow
Was allowed around your pillow.

While you were sleeping peacefully
I prayed for your soul faithfully.
And from your foggy horizon
I saw a change in your season.

While you were sleeping I made room
For a tomorrow free of gloom.
It can be yours just by asking,
Along with so, so many things.

While you were sleeping I rehearsed
The vow I took the very first
Time ever I heard your sweet voice.
For then, stricken, I knew my choice

While you were sleeping I became,
Hand picked by your escort of dames,
Your ardent knight, your chosen one,
Trained never to leave you alone.

Right by your side therefore I'll stay.
I will be your knight come what may.
With love and with fierce loyalty
I'll guard you from adversity.

Letter To a Lady

I hope you understand that this form of courtship
Is as foreign to me and far from being cheap.
I could send you roses backed up by chocolate
Just like the major crowd; I know you'd appreciate.

But think of all the dirt you'd have around your house,
All the pounds you'd put on, also the little mouse.
But maybe you're special, in a class by yourself,
Maybe you expect more from someone like myself.

In order to write you all the poems you will read
And hoping you'll give me something for my good deed,
I can offer you thoughts and they would go like this:
You can start be weighing all the movies I'd miss

And the risks to my health that comes with this homage:
Prostate, hemorrhoids…I can go down a page.
Though this sheer imagery can get you to crack up
I hope it stirs in you something more down than up.

Your heart, my sweet lady, your heart, don't go too far,
Your heart that I longed for, your heart, my magic star.
Then you should consider what you get in return,
All the great benefits that come to you in turn.

First you would get to know thoroughly your lover,
It's often primordial when you live together.
I could lie but so much and the things that I wrote
Besides making you laugh, my character, denote.
Then one day, if you pray, I will, like all of those,
With rose and chocolate, I will write you in prose.

Love Bug

I don't care what they say or do,
Love will lead us the whole life through.
Its power we cannot define,
Will keep us safe, your hand in mine.

Who would have thought over the phone,
One could distinguish his loved one?
But always, our bewildered eyes,
The Lord, with His Might, mesmerize'.

Who would have thought, in the whole world,
So full of all these lovely girls,
Who would, to make my dream come true,
I'd have to recourse to Cebu?

Ask can it be true possibly,
I for certain feel it deeply;
Love has safely lead me to you,
I don't care what they say or do.

Love's Reply

I'll try to be the one you ask
To stay by your side come what may,
The one who gladly takes the task
Of minding you, day after day,

Lovingly cradles all your dreams,
Even those that don't include me,
Patiently listen to your schemes,
Advises when you ask only.

I'll be there at every sunrise
To try to ease your stressy day,
And just before you close your eyes,
Gently takes you to Heaven's way.

No, no you won't have to worry,
I'll be here till the Lord permits
And I'll love you stronger chérie,
Long after He calls my spirit.

Loving You

I'll love you forever no matter where you are.
I'll love you forever, be you near, be you far.
I'll love you forever, which is what I live for.
I'll love you as in life; I've never loved before.

My heart has forever beaten to your cadence,
It remains ectopic without your pure radiance.
I'll love you forever, until you leave our midst,
I'll love you long after you'd have ceased to exist.

Magic Touch

I often sit alone, slowly just taking in
The silent euphoria surging from deep within
When thoughts of you emerge, in a blissful sudden,
Relieving magically whatsoever burden.

You come so silently and with your gentle touch,
Always without a clue, to give ease to my rush.
There, alone in this truce, I feast on the meaning
Of how much I love you and many other things.

But the thoughts I harbor, to one thing often lead:
How lucky I've become since my psyche you feed.
Love has landed in me the day I first met you,
You have planted in me the seed of love so true.

You are my Eureka, the genie of my lamp,
No wonder on my mind so frequently you tramp.
When I feel invaded by this loving feeling,
That's when I sit alone and slowly take all in.

Melancholy

The door swings wide open
And the sun permeates
Down to the empty plates
We dined in so often.

Far in the sky you see
The lengthy trail of clouds
Left weekly by the proud
Air force dignitaries.

Upon the mountain tops,
Shining loud, shining red,
The villas haughty stead
Shows the pride of their props.

And since it's almost ten
You will hear moo the cows
Which an hour will plow
Wishing for eleven.

See how nothing has changed;
The wind bends the branches,
The rain the birds, drenches
But only have estranged

The roses you planted
From this forsaken place.
Like you they left no trace,
Not at all contented…

Funny how without fail,
With deepest displeasure,
The ones you so treasure
Away from your docks sail…

Mind Games

The silent sounds of my reverie
Leave me deaf, distraught and weary
With your name as a seal chérie,
In my cubicle.

There I get all drunk and mellow,
After I drown all my sorrow,
Hearing of your voice the echo,
And my knees buckle.

In no hurry they resurface
To perturb my heart steady pace;
The previous ones leaving no trace
Of my emotions.

For the silence of my dreamland
Will remain hushed up and pretend
That you and I will work as planned;
Sheer apprehension.

Mother

To you I send these lines written in gratitude,
Reflecting all the love I feel for you tonight.
When I recall my sweet infancy, I delight
For it's your smile I see in all its plenitude.

From the day I was born you kept watch over me.
While reserving for you the cup of bitterness
Mother, you always gave to me the very best.
Leading me by the hand, I was too unsteady.

I believe in your love with faith almost divine
And you gave of this love even in darkest days.
It came strong and steady, never failed, never swayed
And even far away its rays over me shined.

You taught me right from wrong and knew, guardian angel,
To preserve my meek heart. And while keeping your cool
Fought against all my odds. And when I was a fool
Still you were wise and knew how to save me from hell.

Mother is the sweet word spoken by the suckling,
Mysterious utterance, source of delectation,
When the soul young again, still missing his Zion,
Holds the pressing desire to express his feelings.

My Bestest

I will simply attempt to tell
Of the grasp you have over me.
How, when kept safe under your spell,
My heart behaving jitterily,
Keeps me so deprived of my rest.

Whenever you decide to come
And gently nudge my starving soul,
I can never, never fathom
How quickly I lose all control
Causing chaos within my chest.

It's always so hard to foresee
When or where it is you'll decide
To come and easily fetch me
Whenever from your hold I glide,
Trying to evade from your nest.

For every single time you call
My whole world simply becomes still
And again on my knees I fall
To receive from you my love fill,
From you, by far, my love dearest.

My Dear One

You, the one I long for,
Long deep within the core,
Can you feel its fierce pace
Missing your sweet embrace?

It throbs as to rejoice
At the sound of your voice,
Then ends in a flutter
When you leave thereafter.

I try so hard to quell
Its all quivering spell
But the sound of your name
Makes it react the same.

This lovely sounding name
Within me, seems to tame
My poor heart's refusal
To love you, my Chantal.

So every word you say
Carries my mind away
And every thought that may
Pulsates my mind astray.

But for so many times
It answered to love chimes;
Some lovely you could tell,
Others sounded like knell.

But for you my jolie
It wakes up suddenly;
Like the sun on my night,
You dissipate my fright.

You I long to embrace
But does not feel the pace
Of the beat of my heart,
Will you tear it apart?

My Grace

In the blank stillness of my night,
You come steady, you come solely.
From deep within my silent plight
I long for your hand, my lovely.

Nothing has ever felt so warm,
Nothing so far's been so mellow,
Nothing can my anger disarm
Better than your sweet voice echo.

The love you feed on the wire
Comes rushing down into my veins.
It ignites this blazing fire
Consuming me, heart, spirit, brain.

It keeps me warm when nights are cold,
Gives me great strength to carry on,
Provides a cozy but strong hold
When my spirit feels like a ton.

You come but one never knows how
You will affect me on that day.
But rest assured, before you bow,
Easily you dispel my gray.

And delighted by the effect
I go on singing through my day.
The infusion is so direct
That nothing can get in its way.

So from the depths of my cold night
I come again to kiss your hand
And suddenly it's warm and bright,
Something the world can't comprehend.

My High Noon

Like the desert under high noon
I burn in the wait of your love
Hoping that it would be here soon
To gladly brighten my alcove.

You spread your wings over my soul
And in my chest where it simmers,
My love, all robed in red and gold,
Over my world spreads its glimmers.

You'll never guess what has become
My whole life caught within your sphere.
You'll never guess just how gruesome
My heart can be without you, dear.

Amidst the treasures I cherish
Your face shines like the purest gold.
With kisses daily I polish
The best asset that I behold.

Like the desert under high noon
You consume my heart from above.
I will remain under your rune
Patiently waiting for your love.

My Jewel

One day I will reveal to you,
When I myself will understand,
The connection between us two
And its origin, as it stands.

I am baffled, puzzled and lost;
Searching always for rationale,
But my meek mind can't pay the cost
To merge into the spiritual.

It's mesmerizing, it's thrilling
That we're allowed, us so afar,
While we are truly just budding,
To reach as high as a bright star.

Over the souls of good lineage
The Chronos displays no power.
So of our book, the early page
Adorns the most precious flower.

Then on that day when I am told
About the nature of our love,
In my arms my jewel I will hold
Truly thinking the Lord above.

My Loving Child

I'll always be around
If it's a wish for you,
Come where always abounds
The Peace to your soul due.

I will lessen your load,
I will give you courage.
If too long is the road
I'll be your Entourage.

You should never despair
When things don't go your way;
What to you may seem fair
Often leads you astray.

Hope, hope in My Goodness,
Bring your least desires.
This show of faithfulness
Sets My Love on fire.

May My Peace be with you
To wash away your frown
And when your dream comes true,
Remember, I am around.

My Pumpkin

Burning up in the love you give,
Melting from the care I receive,
Is the ever-blissful torture
Imposed on me by your rapture.

Why would I flee from your embrace?
Why would I untangle your lace?
Why, while the world and its richness
Bling-bling next to you, my princess?

My Sunrise

This morning I held you so tight,
I could not, just could not let go.
I did not dream of you last night
But today it's one-woman show.

My pillows annoyed by this scene
Did not cradle this déjà vu.
They think you're far, far, not yet seen,
They think... because they miss you too.

It was so strong, it was so real,
It was the best I've ever had,
It was the way you made me feel
That left me stirred but left me sad.

So I got up and naturally
On paper I let run my thoughts.
What is written is meant solely
To let you know how much I'm caught

In this early one-woman show,
Following my long, lonely night.
There I meet my little swallow
And get to hold her so, so tight.

My Treat

Come, my sweet baby, come,
Come rest your weary feet.
Up and down, time and some,
You've been with my spirit.

My mind remains under
The control of my will
But my spirit hovers
Ocean, valley and hill.

It follows you always,
Worries when you don't smile,
Watches over your ways,
Stays with you all the while.

You remain of my dreams
The skillful conductor
And in my days, it seems,
The symphonies linger.

What a divine feeling
To have you as insight.
You keep my day gleaming,
Inspire my deep night.

Come then, my jolie, come,
Come here and be my treat.
Too long I was lonesome,
My soul, come and complete.

My Wife

I prayed and prayed
For a beautiful wife
To cast away
The sadness of my life

Just when I thought
My dream would not come true,
Sad and distraught
I looked up; there were you.

So here I am, I come to you,
My soul on its knees, comes anew,
Begging like a child in distress
For its due share of happiness.

My Zocke

All the loving words I call you,
All my glances so full of clue
Come from a font of heartfelt love
That I know fits you like a glove.

See if I tell you I love you
And I caress you with my vue,
It's just a return of the care
You have on my heart as a snare.

Ode To My Marijune

Just like the sun upon my sphere,
The thoughts of you come bright and clear
And they bud in the depths of me
A crave for your hand, my Junie.

Never in my life has it been,
Never, repeatedly I screened,
Never has it been that I long
For any living soul that long.

My morning sun seems weak and dull,
The moonlight my dreams, just can't lull,
The seasons come and bring new songs
But you air rings ever so strong.

Many mornings my tears I brunch,
But my pillow they always drench
Cannot echo your lovely voice
When your dear name becomes sweet noise.

On My Knees

On my knees I remain,
O Lord of land and sea,
On my knees, to obtain
A glimpse of Your Mercy.

O Lord of days of old
Watch on us carefully
For the loads of our souls
Weigh us down and weary.

In the course of our life
We try hard to prevail.
But this non-ending strife,
Your exams, makes us fail.

You have in many ways
Taught us of the wisdom
That always he, who prays,
To him comes Your Kingdom.

Therefore, O Lord of hosts,
Look down on Your creatures
Who to everyone boast
Of Your Love they treasure.

One Day

One day out of the clear blue,
One day that we did not perceive,
One day like the ones in Cebu,
One day my love I will receive.

One day I'll hold her in my arms,
One day I'll call a blessed day.
One day, beholding all her charms,
One day of lovely month of May.

One day we'll sit just to take in
The true meaning of love divine.
One day, for then through thick and thin,
One day she'll put her hand in mine.

One day therefore we'll know for sure
That once you're led by the good Lord,
You feel confident and secure
That always your day is restored.

One day out of the clear blue,
One day then, right before your eyes,
One day tailored for me and you,
One day you will silence my sighs.

Out Of Time

In short breaths comes the life we live,
It never ceases till it's time,
That time we hear the divine chime,
Right before going through God's sieve.

Be mindful of the breaths we take,
They leave stains the Lord can't erase.
Invest so to avoid the blaze,
Take aim so to the bliss partake.

Overdue

Come step into this very life
That's bound to bloom under your touch.
Come now, my dear, there's no more strife,
I yearn for your brown eyes too much.

The time we spend so far away
While it marinates both our souls,
It levels for us a smooth way
Leading us safely to be whole.

You'll be the flower of my spring,
The songbird of my rainy day,
You'll be the sun brightly shining,
Chasing my cloudy days away.

Your dawning treasures that I seek
Are only offered in due time.
Whereas the dusk I bring is meek,
At times even not worth a dime.

But yet the love that I harbor,
Queuing my many mirages,
Blindfoldedly chose your candor
Amid those lovely visages.

So come, my baby, step right in,
Come step into your new kingdom.
No high, no low, no thick, no thin;
All is leveled for you to come.

Sleepy Debate

Oh God, I am so weary
That I can barely see!
I should be in my bed,
Not seated here instead
With my eyelids of lead
And my eyes blood shot red.

I try hard to relate
This here world to my fate.
Maybe I will succeed
With some unusual speed
To transfer on paper
What I have to offer…

But little do you know,
There's always tomorrow
Coming with a vengeance,
Not giving any chance
To my tired body
Half asleep already…

Why give to the morrow
Part of today's sorrow?
Finish what you started,
Even if ill-fated
But don't go to your bed
Till your thoughts have all sped.

Soul Purging

I can't even begin, with any given words,
Of the healing of soul, to stress the benefits.
But yet my mere attempt will probably be heard
By many or the few, laden with demerits.

To try to shed some light on the matter at hand,
The picture I suggest may be painful at first.
But it will for certain help us to comprehend
The theme I want to treat before I die and burst.

See what's of the body after the soul departs;
Nothing but a mere lump of disgusting decay.
Come then and fully grasp the truth known from the start;
The powerhouse of life is the soul, should I say.

It is therefore fitting that to a strong body,
More than anything else, is needed a strong soul.
In every human being, one the other carries,
In every human being they form a precious whole.

So the every day bond between two human beings,
Before it's physical, emanates from beyond.
It lies deep in the realm of a much-valued thing;
A strange affinity to which we must respond.

So when it so happens that this bond is broken,
For the many reasons so justified today,
What, to the sheer reason, can really be the end,
For the souls left in pain, is a cause for dismay.

The trauma experienced is always felt both ways
Be it amicable or nasty a break up.
It tears you up inside, devours, come what may,
The heart where it resides, its carnal envelope.

So to the soul in pain a needed time of rest
Is rather primordial for it to bond again.
You have to grow back strong, restore your bleeding chest
In order to, one day rid yourself of this stain.

Therefore the soul purging is a much-needed task
Beneficial to both, the body and the soul.
This convalescent time, if well suffered, can mask
Any trace of trauma, any scar, any toll.

It offers the patient a chance to love anew,
Also let them perceive at least a bright future.
When coupled with prayers, the serum strong and true,
It gives them wings to fly right into the azure.

For the spirit in us is willing and able
To soothe deep in the soul whatever was sustained.
He will gently restore, cuddle, even cradle
The meek and moping soul, rid it from pain and stain.

Sweet Apology

I brought you roses, though perishable,
They are to many the most palpable
Of love expression.
I brought you roses, although standing here,
I don't really know if you want to hear
Of my confusion.

I'd say I love you, but of this you're sure
And though you respond with feelings so pure
I know that you doubt of our tomorrow;
You were hurt again, still fresh your sorrow.

If the Lord above decides to ignore
Or fails to bless us, for which I implore,
We will forever quarrel then depart
Then after a while seek each other's heart…

Let us in pure wisdom be with one another
And give the final word to the Lord, our Savior.

Talk Tome, Talk

And peacefully I shut the phone
After I slowly took all in.
Other sound in the room, there's none
Then my mind glides freely within
To contemplate the calm effect
Obtained by the sound of your speech,
It came flowing and so direct
As if you weren't so out of reach.

The miles are many between us,
And the ocean so deep and blue
But this bond remains so obvious,
The shackle binding me to you.
But all the while I so remained
Swallowing your words willingly,
The inner buzz that I obtained
Eludes your mind so teasingly.

And to your repeated "hello's"
To make sure that I am on the line
Bring to me the lovely echo
Of this voice that I find so fine.
Oh talk to me, say anything,
Ignore that I remain silent,
Keep the flow of these words coming,
Being rude is not my intent.

It just that when I talk to you
At any given time of day
I receive the same pure and true
Gift I had for the Holidays...
You will always bring to my ears
Your sound of the loveliest chime
And so for the rest of our years
Will thrill my poor soul anytime.

The Day After

The plane will touch down the concrete
And every one will be relieved.
They'll finally move on their feet,
And gladly will roll up their sleeves.

I will emerge pretty sleepy
From such an ordeal of a trip.
But inside I'll be so happy
That my poor heart will make a flip.

I will emerge quite hesitant
And will begin to screen the hall,
Trying just like a debutant
To find my right mate in this ball.

And finally I will see you,
Meeting all my expectations.
We will go on to start anew
Our true basics of creation.

Then will begin the day after
The first time I will see your face.
It will be by so far better
Than anything I've ever chased.

My sun will regain its true shine,
The rain will never bother me.
Since I will have your hand in mine
Even the cold will be balmy.

My world as a whole will emerge
From this destiny thereafter,
Our lives in one then will converge
Freely, gladly, the day after.

The Gentle Buzz

The gentle buzz I feel inside
When I think of you naturally,
The gentle buzz that love provides
Says I'm in love mercilessly.

The gentle buzz is what I feel
Each and every time on my mind,
Your name comes rolling down on wheels
And land softly, my heart to bind.

It's always so automatic,
Though some might think that it's all planned;
Of your name the gracious music
Gives my heart a stroll on the sand.

The gentle buzz that I treasure
Rolls downs straight from your jolly voice
To stir my heart beyond measure
Even if given other choice.

The gentle buzz therefore will stay
Within my chest as a signal
That finally you came my way
And for my search it's "point final".

The Little Girl And The Piano

She sits erected as she's taught,
Looking at the shinny keyboard.
The focus tempering her thoughts
Is heard in all of her accords.

It's been a hard and lengthy week,
Spent on this so challenging piece.
The perfect form she always seeks,
Slowly but surely led to this.

And so she repeatedly plays,
Ignoring the small world around.
Unaware that in subtle ways
She's shaping her life safe and sound.

The concentration so rehearsed
Later will be her best asset.
For, in her life widely dispersed,
The sense of discipline she'll get.

So painfully she shapes and forms
Her unforeseeable tomorrow
While every note she now deforms,
Her mentor silent tantrum, throws.

The Month Of Angels

When nature finally unravels her beauty
For so long kept unsung, for so long kept in sheaves,
When the sun seems to be so daring and haughty
And every living thing regains the will to live,

When the flowers again open up lovingly
To offer all the birds sample so hard to choose,
From fragrance, shapes and shades presented randomly,
Bewildered eyes to see and troubled souls to soothe,

That's when I think of you, for from my horizon,
The spirit in the air brings me the scent of you.
The month of May begets the best of the season
And sets a lovely stage for love to spring anew.

The month of all mothers remains the mother month
Which seems to be the door of all nature treasures.
The month of all mothers, always from its mere trough,
Daily brings up the world to summertime pleasures.

Always mother knows best so from rain come flowers.
And with the sun warming the birds sing cheery tunes.
But the best gift of all, free from scattered showers,
Of mother month of May comes precious month of June.

For long, so long ago, before the dawn of time,
They carefully ponder over your month of birth.
It was among it all; warm sun, flowers, bird chimes
That it was decided to send you here on Earth.

So when the month of May comes with all its fanfare
And when nature adorns her precious apparel,
They tell the universe tenderly to prepare
For peaceful month of June, famous month of angels.

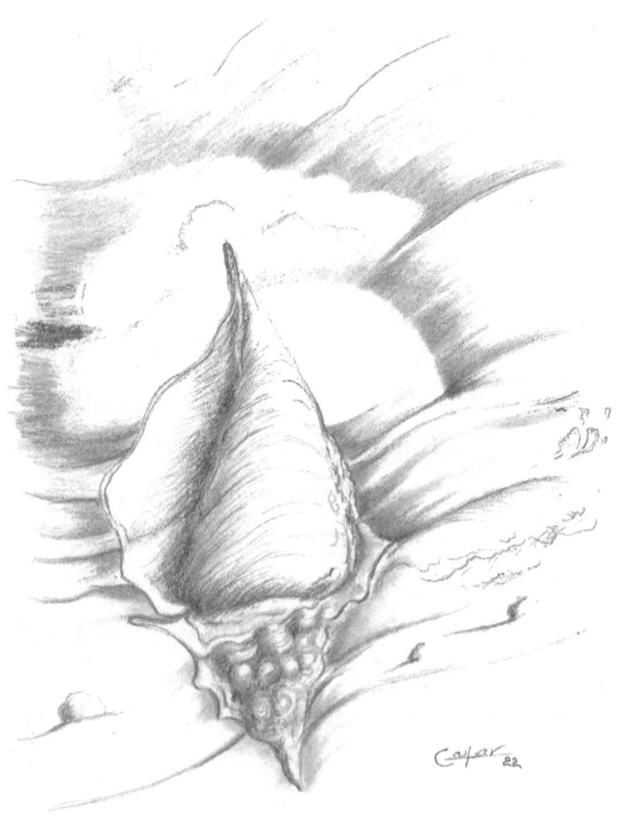

The Package

Along with all you will receive,
In a red box you'll find my heart.
Just be gentle as you retrieve
It; the content may fall apart.

I sent to you my hopes and dreams,
The ones kept always close to me.
They come infused of one main scheme;
To make you mine, my sweet Tome.

I sent also my well wishes,
All that is good and pure and true.
I hope they fill all your misses,
The ones that make your brown eyes blue.

And so I sent you all that's good;
My heart, my spirit and my soul.
My mind and body stayed to brood
Here till with you, we become whole.

The Walk

I could go through this journey
Missing my Heaven daily,
Could be of the common kind
Whose hearts seem to be so blind
But who instead have chosen
On the dark side to remain.
So they exercise the right
To worship the dark world might
Carefully finding reasons
To justify their actions
And pestering rights galore
For their weakness we deplore.
They feel one has to be nut
In life to bear a cross…but

I will walk through my journey
Loving my Lord earnestly,
Leaving for Him all behind,
Seeking Him while I may find
The teachings that He explain'
And within His grace remain.
Keeping in mind that the fight
Is to spare me from the plight
Of losing my God's Zion,
Drifting to oblivion

The blood that He shed before
Runs again as an encore
Each time His children lend not
Their ears to the Love He taught.

"Thou Shall Not"

The laws, it seems,
Are outdated.
Seek grace through Him,
Jesus stated…

But

God gave the laws,
Graces to reap.
Now Grace He sows
The laws to keep.

Then Came You

I once had a girl
As rare as a pearl
Who, could with her smile,
Make you walk long miles.

I once had a girl
Who came in my world
And put in my heart
The fright from the start.

But there I remained
Much more than a friend,
Caught right in her game
And full of my shame.

But along the way
From her web I strayed.
My life made no sense,
Ridded of romance.

I lived through sad days,
Cried my nights away
Alone with the plight
Of dark, empty nights.

Then shone from afar
A glimpse of a star
And to my surprise,
Right before my eyes

Stood cute and lovely,
Subtle yet friendly,
The angel God sent
To heal my complaint

And restore in me
Peace and harmony.
I once had a girl
With her mind in curls

Who left me stranded,
Just flat disbanded…
There's always a prize
After you're chastised.

So to my purpose,
With no cheap disguise,
Just to my rescue
Came someone like you.

This Life

This life you claim to live,
Over all the Earth sown,
This life you once received,
This life is not your own.

One bright and sunny day
It will be asked of you.
Worked so that, come what may
To your heart you be true.

For there, in the stillness,
Only there you'll receive,
Free from riddle and stress,
Cues that are meant to give

Guidance in strives ahead.
So live this life borrowed
With laughter or tears shed,
This precious life you owe.

To A Fellow Nurse

Lord in Your law is in display:
Care for your brethren today.
Twas said to us one day,
Mind the less fortunate. Obey!
To the unlucky in wealth, come what may
Even when you have nothing,
Try to give an offering.
Mind the ones, who are meek,
Be kind to their lack of richness,
Please be mindful of their weakness.

But to us it seems that You say
Care for your brethren today.
It's recalled to us every day.
Mind the less fortunate, You say.
To the unlucky in health, as they say
Even when it's tiring
Give them of your wellbeing.
Mind the ones who are sick
Be kind to their lack of fitness,
The Lord will show you His kindness.

From my mother,

Tomorrow

When the winter of life tomorrow will have shed
Its snow, and a lifetime will have aged the forehead,
We will walk you and I to that destination,
Towards the final stage of the Lord's creation.

Then to you, my soulmate, I will turn my weak sight
And I will love you more, with more power and might
Than the days of our youth, when the spring of this life
Was blooming, and our sun was still high on its path.

Serene and contented, like the meek laborer
From a hard day of work to the cozy fire
Of his peaceful cottage making a slow return,
To the Lord's firmament we will set our concern.

We'll discuss peacefully, the way that souls whisper,
About eternal shores where those who delivered
Hope, faith and charity and would have loved the most,
In justified reward, joyfully can accost.

Under Your Spell

The song you sang to my Master
Got Him helpless under your charms.
In return, He then ministered
And brought my soul into your arms.

So here I am forever yours,
All too resigned, all so happy.
This chase will soon come to a close.
We'll touch hands; it won't be sappy.

And so it will reveal to all,
Despite slips, tumbles and all odds,
That love always stands straight and tall
Around those who put trust in God.

My love for you will not falter.
It grew solid from your absence.
My heart became ever fonder
Slowly simmered in your essence.

Never will I in my lifetime,
Never, for I looked all over,
Never will I, in this lifetime,
Feel like this for any other.

Where It Lies

From the heart where it lies
The love we share watches.
It records tears and sighs,
Even giggles, catches.

If we are all aware
Of the power given,
This blessed love we share
Rises as though leaven'.

It tickles the spirit,
Renders the mind alert,
Sweeping you off your feet,
Makes you an extrovert.

For this deep love we share,
More than ever precious,
Brings to us from up there
That sweet Love of Jesus.

It gives sense to your life,
Makes you jolly and strong,
Helps you in daily strife
Between all rights and wrongs.

Why

The rain and all its drenchedness
Has failed to wash your innocence.
You remained unstained – no offence -
Nothing could upset your kindness.

The cold and all its bitterness
Has failed to freeze your gentle heart.
It remained gracious, set apart,
Fervent amid all this madness.

The sun and all its scorchedness
Has failed to parch your compassion.
You remained the only lesson,
Straight from the good book of sageness.

So tell me then why my fondness,
This flame burning me deep within,
Failed to ignite, from your being,
The ardor fueling your caress?

The wind and all its forcefulness
Has blown away the silent vows,
The ones we understood somehow,
Unspoken from lack of witness.

Surely the world and its madness
Will throw us its intemperance.
It is, my dear, for us a chance
To gain more in devotedness.

Your Dream

Slowly pacing my dear, you were lost in your dream.
Silently my sweet child, as steady as a crown,
On your virgin forehead, without the least of frown,
I put a loving kiss while your gaze remained dim.

Suddenly you shivered, furious and so upset,
In your eyes I could see the thunder drawing near.
The coldness of your stare summoning me to fear,
And the tears on your face causing my heart to fret.

Tears of a virgin heart, tears of a virgin soul,
With deep consternation I observed you roll down,
Tried desperately not to in my own tears go drown,
Atoning in my heart for this love crime in whole.

O my loving angel, please, forgive my weak scheme.
To breathe the air you breathed, feel the silk of your skin,
These are the reasons I, your private world within,
Stepped just to steal a kiss, while still lost in your dream.

Your Face

The look I detect in your eyes
Can brighten up the darkest skies.
The glow surging right from your stare
Reveals a soul candid and fair.

The love behind this childish face
Of my heartbeat, changes the pace.
It brings a calming, inner peace
And my sadness I just dismiss.

The thoughts of your perfect forehead
Are pictured warm and kind instead.
They come down rushing in my mind
To meet mates they finally find.

O Johanna, O Johanna,
You my God sent, you my manna,
Come and sustain the soul in me,
Come and just set my spirit free.

Bryles

And every now and then
When life gets so boring,
Every so now and then
My spirit flies soaring

Towards you, come what may,
O vixen I adore.
You who though far away
Fill me with so much more

Than the physical realm
Would ever dare sustain.
Gently you overwhelm
Every inch of my strain,

Permeate my inner being,
Gild all my heart's desires,
When my soul's wearying
Fill me with love's fires…

Shore of my horizon,
Safe Island of rescue,
Dear flag of my nation,
Treasured lot I pursue,
Come give sense to my days,
Dear angel sent my way.
As would say Aragon,

The Poets

I don't know what comes over me
And compels me to shout out loud,
Not with a shred of infamy
Or with a sense of feeling proud,
What is stirring deep within me.

He who sings only bawls away
Like an unrestrained animal
But from within me, come what may,
There is nothing paranormal;
This the majority can say.

Machado died away from Spain,
His so belovéd land of birth
But with his pen he tried in vain
This cancer to rid from his turf
But up to now, he feels the pain.

Way above the sea and the plains,
Way above mountains and valleys,
Full throttle you can hear complain
Horderlin healthy mentally
And the ever-sober Verlaine.

Marlowe, do not go in the pub,
You won't find Faust but your demise.
Against all the shoulders you rub
Many are devils in disguise
Sent out your cleverness to rob.

Stardust are blessings from the sky
Falling on Earth to light the way
And the Heavens will cry on high
Their slaughter, in painful dismay,
But the world never hears the sighs.

Misery's mother of all dreams,
They come gushing by sadness fed,
The more it hurts, the more you scream
And at the end the light that's shed
Is much brighter as it all seems.

I don't know what come over me
And compels me to shout out loud,
Not with a shred of infamy
And with no sense of feeling proud
What is stirring deep within me.

May 17ᵗʰ

Before that golden day, before the spring left us,
Right before went away that sky of crimson dusk,
In as much Heaven's love on us men, was beset;
Along you came my dove, sheer boredom to offset.

Miracle of this kind rarely do we witness,
You came, love on your mind, vixen of Venus' nest.
Lavishly you bestow, with your silky candor,
Evenly to fellows, your charms, your main treasure…
So to the Creator we give praise in clamor.

First Date (End)

...But if instead our looks express
Loving kindness and tenderness
And we suddenly realize,
Looking into each other's eyes
That round us time seems to stand still
While our hearts feel sweetly ill...

Then maybe baby, just maybe,
The Lord of lords, the Almighty
Must have looked upon us and smiled,
Decided to end that exile
He put my heart so long ago
Solely to repair undergo.

Does it seem too early to see
You've entered my life already?

So come, my God sent child, then come,
Come quickly for I'm so lonesome...

If this seem to be written
With purpose to entertain,
Hopefully it will retain
The full meaning I intend.

Hang In There

After mirages, illusions
And all bad surprises in store,
Surely the rest of the seasons
One day, your karma, will restore.

But you will have to hang in tough,
Steadily keep eyes on your dreams.
I know the ride can be so rough
But I hear the least of your screams.

Along the way you will meet friends
Who will come bring you My solace.
On this parched and deserted land
There'll be oasis to embrace.

Do not ever force any door
That refuses to be opened.
What is truly yours from the core
Will gladly slide right in your hand.

But soon enough, oh soon enough,
Your karma will know better score.
Despite desert so dry and rough,
Soon it will shine just as before.

Your Love

And finally, oh finally,
Out of dark and stormy skies,
What I hoped for so eagerly
Came crashing right before my eyes.

It came like an awaited dawn,
Like a tornado in winter.
It came and landed on my lawn
Then nudged my too foggy thinker.

How is it that I failed to grasp
This so obvious repeated plea?
Was I entangled in a clasp
Of greener grass my eyes could see?

It came and right then I perceived
This awesome treasure I beheld.
It came and right there I received
This lovely blow below the belt.

You have been there through thick and thin,
Never wavering in your care.
You stood aside so to let in
Whosoever was my affair.

You carried it so many years,
And did not once lose of your zest.
And then shed just as many tears
For every stranger that I test'.

Honestly I tried to connect
With this shadow carrying me
But sadly I failed to respect
Of your brown eyes the loving plea.

So now I kneel before your strength,
Give in to your perseverance.
Your patience was used at great length,
Now you deserve more than a chance.

You loved me with your heart and mind,
Were always there when times were rough.
I know that for now on I'll find
My best mate in peak or in trough.

The love you offer I worship
For it favors that of my Lord.
In my embrace I want to keep
This treasure I can now afford.

Therefore I say it right out loud,
As to thank the highest Heaven
And to warm the upcoming crowd,
That I love you, you my best friend.

Graduation Wishes

Now that you're all imbued,
So well trained and subdued,
Here is the final score
That'll make you think some more.

You'll wish in days ahead
You'd learnt typing instead,
Not pharmacology,
Nor child delivery.

But then the best of deals,
Finally you will steal.
Since you'll be underpaid
Your sweat will be repaid;
God, His angels indeed,
Rewards for every deed.

Honor, Praises and Glory

To the greatest act of Love
Christians come on bended knee,
Join your tears to the tale of
His sufferings for the so many.
Since it is for our offenses
That the Lord suffers today,
Melted by His sufferances
Live and die following His way.

Kneeling in the garden alone
Deep within He suffers the strife,
HE fears, hopes and prays His prone,
Begging: "Father, please spare my life!"
At times the fear envelops Him,
At time love seems the only choice,
But finally love's divine scheme
Rings aloud with a stronger voice.

Judas possessed, in his wile,
Accosts Him, with infamy.
He kisses Him … and meanwhile
Hands Him to His enemies!
Judas, we get on your trail
Every time we, by our sins,
The beloved Lord we fail
Causing over His sufferings.

HE's abandoned at the mercy
Of a horde of raging demons,
And over His face you can see
The traces of their weapons.
You should have, O angels faithful,
Witnessing their wrongdoing,
Spare Him from this act most awful
Or destroy this throng of fiends.

They dragged Him to the high priest
Who backs up their vile doing,
And raising his cursed fist
Accuses Him of blaspheming.
When He 'll come to judge the world,
This Savior and his justice,
When His thunder will unfurl,
He will accuse you of all this.

As He goes through His ordeal
All conspire to torment Him.
Even Peter losing his zeal
Denied being part of His team
But Jesus pierces his soul
With the most tender of glance,
Since to him this was foretold,
Bitter regrets make him wince.

Before Pilate they compare Him
To a louse though He never was;
Oh! But what a most vile scheme
To Him they choose Barabbas!
But what a dreadful sight to see,
The righteous one's forsaken,
They condemn Him with no mercy
But the crime is forgiven.

So they strip him and they bind Him,
At Him each throws his anger.
And this spotless Lamb now seems
To withstand their blows no longer.
We are all the real victims,
Desist O cruel tormentors!
Come and pour your hatred steam
On us the true perpetrators.

And a wretched crown of thorns
Pierces His most divine head.
To Him archangels adorn,
Worldly thugs, you taunt with stead.
And He languishes in pain,
And suffers down to His soul
But you delight as you spend
Over you glories you extol.

He walks and He climbs Calvary
Laden by this weighty wood:
From there like on pulpit, carries
His voice as loud as He could,
"Father, spare them, I beg of you,
For they know not what they do."
That's for Christians a way brand new
To revenge when they're done unto.

A large mutinous troop shouts
And insulting Him as they scream:
If of this bind He comes out,
Oh yes, we will believe in Him!
Easily He can desist
The torture He undergoes
But He just cannot resist
This great Love His Heart echoes.

Ah! From Your throne of torture
Lord of lords, please do not descend:
By Your power, keep Your tenure,
Remain there until the end.
But please, keep Your solemn promise
And pull us all by Your grace;
So to obtain heavenly bliss
Keep us all in Your trace.

He expires and all nature
In Him mourns the Creator.
On earth there is no one creature
That does not grieve for its author.
Such a terrible spectacle
Would not it melt down my heart?
Unless I am hard to tackle
Like the hardest stone of art.

Mary Magdalene

So she went to the tomb, sent by the other ones,
In the dark early dawn, panting under love prongs,
To see her dead Master.
The shock of the last days and its scarring trauma
Had stamped on her aura a dreadful aroma;
So she walked much faster.

So she got to the tomb and to her sad surprise
The stone keeping it safe was rolled despite its size,
Leaving it gaping wide.
And as she looked inside and saw the emptiness,
Her viscera were torn and she bled in distress;
Sobbing, holding her sides.

No guards to inquire, no one to alleviate
The overwhelming fear that had become her state,
Each breath was hard to take,
Lost in her disarray she perceived the gardener.
"Sir, can you please tell me? ..." missing His demeanor,
Drowning in her heartache.

"Mary" rang in her ears, said by the sweetest voice,
"Don't be sad, it is I", He said with divine poise,
Touched by her grief within,
"Don't hug me but rather go tell my disciples
That I rose as I said, I who makes possible
For men to rise from sin."

By the sound of His voice she knew and was certain
That it was her Master and her joy she regained,
All by His great mercy.
He chose to alleviate the sorrows of her heart,
Knowing her love for Him. So about to depart
He showed her clemency.

So she ran to the rest, brought to them the good news,
Becoming the bearer so joyfully enthused
Of her dear Lord's rising,
Thus gladly erasing the woes that had become
Their lives from the torments from that scene most gruesome;
So they prayed in hiding.

Peter and John took off and reached the tomb's entrance
And as she said they saw, as He said in advance;
His body left the den.
So back to the others they carried what they saw,
Still doubtful they remained, found Mary's story raw,
But were less downtrodden.

But Mary in her heart stirring and full of joy,
Had no doubt she had seen her Master who destroyed
Her demons indwelling
For He who all creates can also elevate,
From any mire pit to beauty, reinstate
His creatures up from sin.

Her mourning has become a great jubilation,
Her sorrow turned into sheer exhilaration,
Like Moses on the mount,
For he saw the Father but her, she saw the Son,
Unequaled in splendor, glowing brightly like none,
Of all good things the Fount.

And He called her "Mary", as He so often did
And the ears of her heart had recalled the splendid
Sound of His blessed voice.
Forever she'll remain His humble news bearer,
The one He first offered relief and a fairer
Outlook for her to rejoice.

He said, "Hurry Mary, go inform the others
So they can gleefully impart to the brothers
The most comforting news.
Tell them death is destroyed, that the tomb is no more,
That I rose to bring life unlike ever before
To all those who so choose."

"That as I said before my yoke is sweet and light,
That I'm ever willing to help them through the fights
In every strife within,
That forever I'm here to chase away their fears
And that all my brethren, who follow me I'll steer,
Raising them from all sin."

Famous Quotes

The devil pays his debts with our emotions.

✫ ⌃ ✫ ⌃ ✫

A nurse is an angel with an assignment;
Some are for hire, others just volunteer.

✫ ⌃ ✫ ⌃ ✫

There is an expiration date
Stamped on my fondest love affairs.
It comes not a minute too late;
When least hoped for, it's in the air.

✫ ⌃ ✫ ⌃ ✫

Forget about you or fondle the sun
Which is easier or which is more fun?

www.ingramcontent.com/pod-product-compliance
Lightning Source LLC
Chambersburg PA
CBHW051833130726
47987CB00002B/526